cooking for kids

Chef express

Published by:
TRIDENT PRESS INTERNATIONAL
801 12th Avenue South, Suite 400
Naples, Fl 34102 USA
Tel: + 1 239 649 7077
Fax: + 1 239 649 5832
Email: tridentpress@worldnet.att.net
Websites: www.trident-international.com
www.chefexpressinternational.com

Cooking for kids

Publishers: Simon St. John Bailey and
Elaine S. Evans
Editor-in-chief: Isabel Toyos

Texts
Editing and supervision: Aurora Giribaldi
Translation: Sandra Heyman
Proofreading: Rosa Corgatelli

Design and lay out
Cover: Matilde Bossi
Inside: M&A Gráfica
Step by step photography: Fernando Giampieri
Step by step styling: Emi Pechar

Prepress
Mikonos Comunicación Gráfica

Includes Index
ISBN 1582796696
UPC 6 15269 96696 9

First Edition Printed in February 2004

Printed in Peru by Quebecor

introduction

In this book you will find wonderful ideas and nourishing options for feeding your children during their school years. Our recipes have a high nutritional content but do not scarify flavor, so they will help you teach your kids about what foods are nutritious and, at the same time, will allow you to create tempting menus for the whole family.

cooking for kids

introduction

How to develop healthy eating habits in your children?

- Always talk to them about good nutrition, and involve them in the preparation of meals.
- Children learn most effectively by following the example of their parents. To promote this, eat together as a family as often as possible.
- Avoid buying sweet biscuits, soft drinks and other "empty energy" (non-nutritious) foods regularly. It is easier to prevent temptation if these products are not kept at home.

What your children need

Food groups	They provide
• *Bread, cereals.*	• *Carbohydrate, fiber, prote vitamins and minerals.*
• *Vegetables, fruits.*	• *Vitamins and fiber.*
• *Fish, seafood, poultry, meat, eggs, dried beans, nuts, seeds.*	• *Protein, vitamins and minerals.*
• *Milk, cheese, yogurt.*	• *Minerals and vitamins, protein.*
• *Butter, margarine or oil.*	• *Vitamins, fat.*

- Always have fruits at home. Children will tend to get into the habit of eating fruit at home if it is available, especially if they see their parents eating it.
- Encourage lots of physical activity to build up healthy appetites and help prevent obesity.
- Serve regular meals –breakfasts, lunch or packed lunches for school, and dinner. Give them small servings and allow them to ask for more.

Minimum daily amounts

- *4-6 servings - 1 slice bread or small bowl breakfast cereal or 1/2 cup pasta or rice.*
- *4-6 servings – 1 piece fruit or 1/2 cup vegetables.*
- *2 servings – 100 g/3 1/2 oz meat or 3/4 cup cooked beans.*
- *600 ml/1 pt milk or 40 g/1 1/2 oz cheese and 200 g/6 1/2 oz yogurt.*
- *1-2 tablespoons.*

Difficulty scale

■□□ | Easy to do

■■□ | Requires attention

■■■ | Requires experience

dried fruit salad with bananas

■□□ | Cooking time: 40 minutes - Preparation time: 10 minutes

method

1. Soak prunes and apricots in water overnight, drain.
2. Place prunes, apricots, sultanas and bananas in ovenproof dish.
3. Combine honey with a little hot water, pour over fruit. Add lemon rind and butter.
4. Cover with foil. Bake in moderate oven 35 minutes.
5. Add orange juice, reheat in oven 5 minutes. Serve hot or cold with yogurt if desired.

Serves 4

ingredients

- **1/4 cup pitted prunes**
- **1/3 cup dried apricots halves**
- **1/4 cup sultanas**
- **3 bananas**
- **2 tablespoons honey**
- **1/2 teaspoon grated lemon rind**
- **15 g/1/2 oz butter, melted**
- **1 cup freshly squeezed orange juice**

tip from the chef

Make ahead if desired. Keep refrigerated.

french toast

■□□ | Cooking time: 5 minutes - Preparation time: 10 minutes

ingredients

- > **1 egg**
- > **1/4 cup milk**
- > **3 slices wholemeal bread**
- > **butter to grease pan**
- > **honey to serve**

method

1. Beat egg and milk together with rotary beater.
2. Cut slices of bread in half. Heat greased frying pan.
3. Pick up bread with a fork and dip both sides into egg mixture.
4. Cook bread in hot pan. Turn when browned underneath. Cook other side until golden.
5. Serve immediately with honey.

Makes 6 slices

tip from the chef

This makes a good breakfast, and it is also great for winter afternoons.

pikelet faces

a

■■□ | Cooking time: 15 minutes - Preparation time: 15 minutes

method

1. Sift flours into bowl, make a well in the center, add milk (a), orange rind, orange juice, oil and butter. Stir until smooth (or process mixture for 1 minute).
2. Place 1/2 cup of the mixture into another bowl, add cocoa (b) and stir until smooth. Spoon cocoa mixture into a piping bag, made with greaseproof paper.
3. Heat extra butter in pan. Pipe eyes and mouth on to pan (c) and leave to cook for 30 seconds. Gently pour a tablespoon of orange mixture on top of the face (d) and continue cooking.
4. Turn pikelet over when bubbles begin to appear. Lightly cook other side and remove from pan. Repeat with remaining mixtures.
5. To make honey butter, stir honey into butter until combined. Serve with pikelets.

Makes about 20

ingredients

- **1 cup wholemeal self-raising flour**
- **1 cup white self-raising flour**
- **2/3 cup milk**
- **2 teaspoons grated orange rind**
- **2 tablespoons orange juice**
- **3 tablespoons oil**
- **30 g/1 oz butter, melted**
- **1 tablespoon cocoa**
- **extra butter, for pan**

honey butter

- **2 tablespoons honey**
- **60 g/2 oz softened butter**

tip from the chef

You can enrich orange mixture with different fruits cut into very small cubes.

b

c

d

fruity slice

■□□ | Cooking time: 25 minutes - Preparation time: 10 minutes

ingredients

- 1 cup sugar
- 250 g/1/2 lb butter
- 1 cup sultanas
- 1 cup chopped apricots (same size as sultanas)
- 2 eggs, beaten
- 1 cup white self-raising flour
- 1 cup wholemeal self-raising flour
- 1 teaspoon mixed spice

method

1. Place sugar and butter in saucepan, heat until butter melts. Add sultanas, apricots and eggs. Mix well.
2. Sift flours into a bowl, return husks to bowl. Stir sifted flours and mixed spice into butter fruit mixture.
3. Spread into greased Swiss roll tin. Bake in moderate oven for 20 minutes.
4. Cool before cutting into squares. Store in airtight container.

Serves 12

tip from the chef

This slice keeps for up to one week, if there is any left.

wholemeal shortbread

■□□ | Cooking time: 40 minutes - Preparation time: 15 minutes

method

1. Beat butter and sugar together with an electric mixer until light and fluffy. Stir in combined dry ingredients in two lots to make a firm dough.
2. Turn dough onto floured surface and lightly knead until smooth, about 2 minutes.
3. Roll out dough to about a 1 cm/1/2 in thickness, and cut into a 20 cm/8 in round. Use thumb and forefinger of one hand and forefinger of the other to pinch edge of shortbread decoratively, if desired.
4. Mark shortbread into 8 equal slices, being careful not to cut right through. Bake in moderately slow oven for 30-40 minutes or until beginning to brown.

Makes 1

ingredients

- **250 g/1/2 lb butter**
- **1/2 cup brown sugar**
- **1 cup wholemeal plain flour, sifted**
- **1 cup plain flour, sifted**
- **1/4 cup rice flour**
- **1/4 cup wheatgerm**

tip from the chef

To asure freshness and avoid dampening, keep it in an airtight container.

cheesy oat burgers

■■□ | Cooking time: 15 minutes - Preparation time: 10 minutes

ingredients

- 1 cup grated cheddar cheese
- 1/4 cup green pepper, finely chopped
- 1 tomato, finely chopped
- 1 small onion, finely chopped
- 1 cup oats
- 2 eggs, lightly beaten
- 1/3 cup plain flour
- oil for frying

method

1. In a medium bowl combine cheese, pepper, tomato, onion, oats, eggs and flour (a); mix well. Divide mixture into 6 small portions (b) and shape into patties (c).
2. Heat oil in a large frying pan, add oat burgers and using a spatula, turn over (d) and cook other side. Cook 3 minutes each side, or until oat burgers are golden.
3. Serve on a wholemeal roll with salad.

Makes 6

tip from the chef

It is important to keep children away from the heat while we are cooking.

a

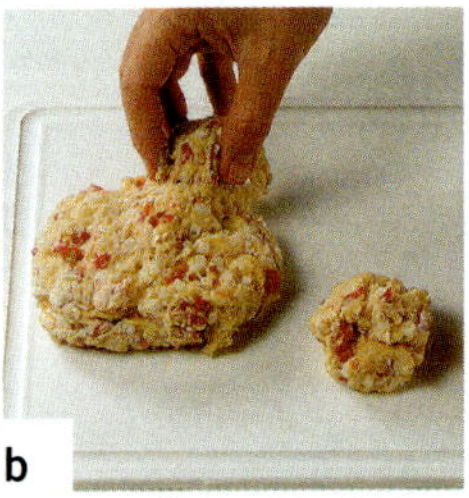

b

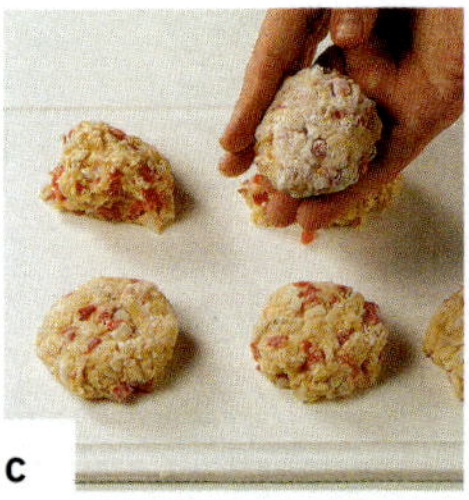

c

d

pizza men

■□□ | Cooking time: 25 minutes - Preparation time: 10 minutes

method

1. Using a man-shaped cutter, cut shapes from bread. Spread shapes with sauce and top with turkey, pineapple, green or red pepper and cheese.
2. Place men on baking trays and bake at 180°C/350°F/Gas 4 for 20-25 minutes or until pizzas are crunchy and golden.

Makes 12

ingredients

- **12 slices bread**
- **90 ml/3 fl oz prepared pizza or tomato sauce**
- **4 slices cooked turkey breast, chopped**
- **125 g/4 oz pineapple pieces, chopped**
- **1/4 green or red pepper, chopped**
- **125 g/4 oz grated tasty cheese (mature Cheddar)**

tip from the chef

With this fun recipe, you can prepare varied shaped pizzas using different cutters.

hi-fiber pasties

■■□ | Cooking time: 30 minutes - Preparation time: 15 minutes

ingredients

- > **2 sheets wholemeal shortcrust pastry**
- > **15 g/$^1/_2$ oz butter**
- > **1 onion, sliced**
- > **1 rasher bacon, chopped**
- > **1 carrot, chopped**
- > **125 g/4 oz canned baked beans**
- > **$^2/_3$ cup grated cheese**
- > **1 egg, beaten**

method

1. Use an upside down saucer to cut out two rounds of pastry.
2. Heat butter in pan, cook onion, bacon and carrot 5 minutes, cool. Add baked beans and mix well.
3. Divide baked beans mixture between pastry circles. Pile filling into center of pastry, sprinkle with cheese. Brush edges with beaten egg, fold over pastry to form a pastie. Make a fluted pattern to seal.
4. Place pasties onto greased oven tray, brush with beaten egg. Bake in moderate oven 25 minutes or until golden brown. Cool, then refrigerate until ready to take to school.

Makes 2

tip from the chef

These are quick and easy to make and very high in fiber. Make the night before.

fruity cheese log

■■□ | Cooking time: 0 minute - Preparation time: 15 minutes

method

1. Soak apricots in orange juice overnight.
2. Blend cream cheese and Cheddar cheese together, stir in apricots and juice mixture. Add peanuts, mix well. Refrigerate for 1 hour.
3. Roll mixture into log shape about 20 cm/8 in long, roll in poppy seeds, cover and refrigerate overnight.
4. Serve with dry crackers, such as wheatmeal or water biscuits.

Serves 4

ingredients

- **70 dried apricots, finely chopped**
- **2 tablespoons orange juice**
- **250 g/$\frac{1}{2}$ lb packet cream cheese**
- **$\frac{1}{2}$ cup grated Cheddar cheese**
- **$\frac{1}{4}$ cup chopped peanuts**
- **$\frac{3}{4}$ cup poppy seeds**

tip from the chef

Make this in advance and keep refrigerated up to a week. This recipe would appeal to gourmet kids.

celery boats

■□□ | Cooking time: 0 minute - Preparation time: 10 minutes

ingredients

- 2 sticks celery
- 1/4 cup cream cheese
- 1/4 cup peanut butter
- sultanas

method

1. Wash celery and trim ends.
2. Beat cream cheese and peanut butter together, spread along groove in celery.
3. Dot with sultanas. Cut into 5 cm/2 in lengths. Place into play-lunch bags and seal.

Serves 2

tip from the chef

These very crunchy and nourishing boats can be served as appetizers in a birthday party.

veal
with tomato and cheese

■■■ | Cooking time: 35 minutes - Preparation time: 20 minutes

method

1. Beat veal steaks until very thin or ask your butcher to do it for you. Dip veal into egg, then coat in combined breadcrumbs and Parmesan cheese.
2. Heat 2 tablespoons oil in pan, cook veal until golden brown on both sides. Drain on absorbent paper. Arrange veal in a single layer in a lightly greased shallow ovenproof dish.
3. Heat remaining oil in saucepan, cook onion 5 minutes, stirring occasionally. Add tomatoes and remaining ingredients except cheese. Cook slowly for 5 minutes. Purée mixture in blender or processor until smooth.
4. Pour tomato sauce mixture over veal, top with cheese slices. Bake in moderate oven 10-15 minutes or until cheese melts and veal is heated through.

ingredients

- **500 g/1 lb thin veal steaks (about 5 medium steaks)**
- **1 egg, beaten**
- **1 cup wholemeal breadcrumbs**
- **1/4 cup grated Parmesan cheese**
- **1/4 cup oil**
- **1 small onion, finely chopped**
- **400 g/13 oz canned tomatoes, undrained**
- **1/4 teaspoon dried basil**
- **1/2 chicken stock cube, softened in 1/4 cup hot water**
- **1 tablespoon tomato paste**
- **1 clove garlic, crushed**
- **small strip lemon peel**
- **6 slices mozzarella cheese**

Serves 4-6

tip from the chef

A good dish to make for guests.

chinese beef stir-fry

■□□ | Cooking time: 15 minutes - Preparation time: 15 minutes

ingredients

- > **500 g/1 lb beef fillet**
- > **1 clove garlic, crushed**
- > **3 teaspoons cornflour**
- > **1 teaspoon soy sauce**
- > **2 tablespoons oil**
- > **3 sticks celery, sliced**
- > **1 small carrot, sliced**
- > **1 tablespoon tomato sauce**
- > **1 teaspoon Worcestershire sauce**
- > **2 tablespoons water**
- > **1 chicken stock cube**
- > **1 tablespoon hoisin sauce**
- > **3 teaspoons barbecue sauce**

method

1. Cut beef into 5 mm/1/4 in slices. Combine garlic, cornflour and soy sauce in bowl, add beef, mix well, stand 20 minutes.
2. Heat pan, add oil; when oil is hot, add beef and cook over high heat until golden brown. Add celery and carrot, cook further 1 minute, remove from pan.
3. Add remaining ingredients to pan, stir over high heat until sauce boils and thickens. Add beef and vegetable mixture, mix well. Serve with brown rice.

Serves 4

tip from the chef

In this typical Oriental dish, beef can be replaced by chicken.

mango chicken

a

■■□ | Cooking time: 80 minutes - Preparation time: 10 minutes

method

1. Cut chicken into 8 pieces (a). Remove skin and visible fat.
2. Heat oil in pan, cook onions 5 minutes, stirring occasionally (b). Add chicken, brown lightly all over.
3. Add mango, nutmeg, lemon rind, combined cornflour and stock and lemon juice (c). Cook, stirring, until mixture boils and thickens.
4. Pour into casserole dish, cover, bake in moderate oven for 1 hour.
5. Stir in yogurt (d). Reheat in oven 5 minutes. Serve with brown rice and salad.

Serves 4

ingredients

- **1 x 750 g/3 lb chicken**
- **1 tablespoon oil**
- **2 onions, sliced**
- **425 g/13 1/2 oz canned mango, drained, puréed**
- **pinch grated nutmeg**
- **3 strips lemon rind**
- **2 teaspoons cornflour**
- **1 1/2 cups chicken stock**
- **1 tablespoon lemon juice**
- **1/2 cup natural yogurt**

tip from the chef

A gourmet plate, great for the children to start trying new kinds of food.

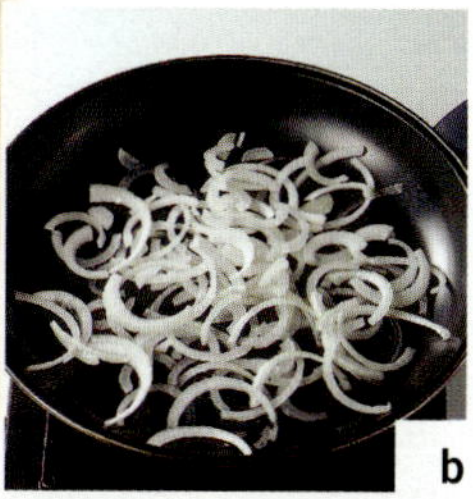

b

c

d

spicy apricot pork fillets

■□□ | Cooking time: 30 minutes - Preparation time: 5 minutes

ingredients

- **500 g/1 lb pork fillets**
- **2 teaspoons cornflour**
- **2 teaspoons soy sauce**
- **1 clove garlic, crushed**
- **2 teaspoons grated fresh ginger**
- **425 g/13 1/2 oz apricot nectar**
- **1/2 teaspoon chili sauce (optional)**

method

1. Place pork fillets in a shallow ovenproof dish.
2. Blend cornflour with soy sauce, garlic, ginger, apricot nectar and chili sauce. Pour over fillets.
3. Bake uncovered in moderate oven 30 minutes.
4. Serve with steamed vegetables and brown rice.

Serves 4

tip from the chef

It is an very quick and easy recipe, ideal to serve as a main meal.

sesame coated chicken

■□□ | Cooking time: 40 minutes - Preparation time: 10 minutes

method

1. Combine tahini, olive and sesame oil and tomato paste on a plate.
2. Coat chicken pieces in mixture, then roll in sesame seeds.
3. Place onto rack in a baking dish. Bake in moderate oven 40 minutes or until golden brown and cooked through.
4. Cool on rack, then refrigerate until ready to use. Place into lunch boxes, serve with bread and butter and salad.

Serves 4-6 (depends on appetites)

ingredients

- **1 tablespoon tahini**
- **2 tablespoons olive oil**
- **1 tablespoon sesame oil**
- **1 tablespoon tomato paste**
- **12 chicken drumsticks and/or wings**
- **2 tablespoons sesame seeds**

tip from the chef

For something different, use soy sauce instead of tahini.

ocean perch in an oven bag

■■□ | Cooking time: 20 minutes - Preparation time: 15 minutes

ingredients

- **2 ocean perch fillets**
- **2 teaspoons mild mustard**
- **1 spring onion, finely chopped**
- **1 orange, rind grated, juice squeezed**
- **1 tomato, sliced**
- **15 g/1/2 oz butter**

method

1. Trim any remaining skin or bones from fish. Arrange in an oven bag in a single layer.
2. Spread each fillet with mustard. Sprinkle with spring onion, grated orange rind and juice.
3. Arrange tomato slices on top. Dot with butter. Seal bag, place in shallow ovenproof dish.
4. Bake in moderate oven 20 minutes. Open bag, use a spatula to lift fish with topping onto plates. Serve with sliced jacket potatoes, brown rice or salad.

Serves 2

tip from the chef

Ocean perch has almost no bones or skin so it is ideal for kids.

tuna fish fingers

Cooking time: 15 minutes - Preparation time: 15 minutes

method

1. Combine tuna, potatoes, parsley, tamari and chutney. Gradually add enough egg to make a moist but not over-soft mixture.
2. Divide mixture evenly into 10 pieces. Form into 1.25 cm/1/2 in thick rectangular fingers. Coat in breadcrumbs.
3. Bake on an oven tray in moderate oven for 10 minutes or until golden. Alternately, grill or shallow fry on both sides until golden.
4. Serve with a salad.

Serves 4

ingredients

- **220 g/7 oz canned tuna, drained, mashed**
- **2 medium potatoes, boiled and mashed**
- **2 tablespoons chopped parsley**
- **1 tablespoon tamari or soy sauce**
- **1 tablespoon chutney**
- **1 egg, beaten**
- **1 cup wholemeal breadcrumbs**

tip from the chef

Freeze fish fingers for up to one month if desired.

vegeroni vegetable bake with cheese

■■□ | Cooking time: 50 minutes - Preparation time: 15 minutes

ingredients

- 250 g/1/2 lb packet vegeroni
- 1 tablespoon oil
- 1 onion, chopped
- 1 carrot, chopped
- 1 stick celery, chopped
- 1 zucchini, chopped
- 1 cup broccoli flowerets
- 400 g/13 oz tomatoes, undrained
- 1/4 cup tomato paste mixed with 1/4 cup water
- 1 clove garlic, crushed
- 250 g/1/2 lb grated mozzarella cheese

method

1. Cook vegeroni in large pot of boiling water until tender, drain, pour into base of shallow ovenproof dish.
2. Heat oil in pan, cook onion, carrot and celery 10 minutes; stirring occasionally. Add zucchini, broccoli, tomatoes, tomato paste and garlic. Cook, stirring occasionally, 20 minutes. Add a little water from time to time to keep it moist. Mixture should not be dry.
3. Add vegetable mixture to vegeroni, mix well. Sprinkle with grated cheese. Bake in moderate oven 10 minutes or until cheese melts and vegeroni are heated through. Serve with salad.

Serves 4-6

tip from the chef

Vegeroni can be replaced by any other pasta you may have available.

salt

vegetable risotto

■■□ | Cooking time: 25 minutes - Preparation time: 10 minutes

method

1. Heat oil in a saucepan over a medium heat, add onion, carrots and mushrooms and cook, stirring, for 3-4 minutes or until onion is soft. Add rice, zucchini and red or green pepper or peas and cook, stirring, for 2 minutes longer.
2. Stir tomato or vegetable juice and stock into mixture and bring to the boil. Reduce heat, cover and simmer for 12-15 minutes or until rice is tender and liquid is absorbed. Sprinkle with cheese and pine nuts or sesame seeds and serve.

Serves 4

ingredients

- **1 tablespoon vegetable oil**
- **1 small onion, chopped**
- **125 g/4 oz carrots, finely diced or grated**
- **60 g/2 oz button mushrooms, sliced**
- **$\frac{3}{4}$ cup/170 g/5$\frac{1}{2}$ oz short-grain rice**
- **90 g/3 oz zucchini, sliced**
- **$\frac{1}{4}$ red or green pepper, sliced or 30 g/1 oz frozen peas**
- **1 cup/250 ml/8 fl oz tomato or vegetable juice**
- **$\frac{1}{2}$ cup/125 ml/4 fl oz vegetable or chicken stock**
- **45 g/1$\frac{1}{2}$ oz grated tasty cheese (mature Cheddar)**
- **toasted pine nuts or sesame seeds**

tip from the chef

Risotto is a typical Italian dish. It can be very nutritious when it includes a variety of ingredients, as in this case.

pea and mushroom flan

■■□ | Cooking time: 50 minutes - Preparation time: 20 minutes

ingredients

flan pastry

- **1 1/2 cups wholemeal plain flour**
- **2 tablespoons finely grated Parmesan cheese**
- **125 g/4 oz butter, chopped**
- **2 tablespoons milk, approximately**

filling

- **2 cups cooked peas**
- **100 g/3 1/2 oz baby mushrooms, sliced**
- **1/2 cup cream**
- **1/2 cup cottage cheese**
- **1 cup grated Cheddar cheese**
- **2 eggs**

method

1. To make pastry, combine flour and cheese in a bowl, rub in butter. Add enough milk to mix to a firm dough. Knead lightly on a floured surface, wrap dough, refrigerate for 30 minutes.
2. Re-roll pastry to fit a 23 cm/9 in flan tin. Cover pastry with grease proof paper, and sprinkle with pastry weights. Cook in a hot oven for 10 minutes. Remove paper and weights and cook for a further 5 minutes.
3. To make filling, spread peas and mushrooms evenly into flan. In a medium bowl combine cream, cottage cheese, half of Cheddar cheese and eggs, mix well. Pour over peas.
4. Sprinkle remaining Cheddar cheese over top and bake in moderate oven 30-35 minutes.

Serves 6

tip from the chef

Serve this flan hot or cold, with green salad.

satay vegetables

■□□ | Cooking time: 10 minutes - Preparation time: 5 minutes

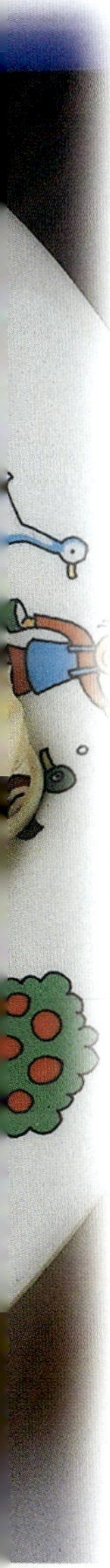

method

1. Heat oil in a frying pan over a medium heat, add snow peas, sweet corn, broccoli, bean sprouts and red pepper and stir-fry for 3 minutes.
2. Add peanut butter, soy sauce and water and cook, stirring, for 4 minutes longer or until vegetables are tender.
3. Serve with rice or noodles.

Serves 2-4

ingredients

- > **2 teaspoons vegetable oil**
- > **12 snow peas, trimmed and halved**
- > **375 g/12 oz canned baby sweet corn, drained**
- > **60 g/2 oz chopped broccoli**
- > **15 g/1/2 oz bean sprouts**
- > **1/4 red pepper, chopped**
- > **1/4 cup/60 g/2 oz peanut butter**
- > **1 tablespoon reduced-salt soy sauce**
- > **1/4 cup/60 ml/2 fl oz water**

tip from the chef

It is a perfect vegetarian dish, quick and healthy.

yogurt treats

■□□ | Cooking time: 0 minute - Preparation time: 5 minutes

ingredients

strawberry yogurt whip

> $1/3$ cup/60 g/2 oz strawberry yogurt
> $1/3$ cup/90 ml/3 fl oz milk
> 4 strawberries
> 2 ice cubes

yogurt pops

> 1 cup/200 g/$6^1/2$ oz fruit-flavored yogurt of your choice
> $1/3$ cup/90 ml/3 fl oz apricot purée
> 2 tablespoons sugar, or to taste (optional)

method

1. To make whip, place yogurt, milk, strawberries and ice cubes in a blender or food processor and process until smooth and fluffy. Pour into a cup or glass and serve immediately.
2. To make pops, place yogurt, apricot purée and sugar, if using, in a bowl and mix to combine. Pour into ice-block (ice-lolly) moulds or ice cube trays, cover loosely with plastic food wrap and freeze for 5 hours or until solid.

Makes 1 whip and 6 pops

tip from the chef

If using ice cube trays, insert a wooden paddle pop (ice-lolly) stick into each cube before mixture freezes solid.

fruity drinks

■□□ | Cooking time: 0 minute - Preparation time: 5 minutes

method

1. To make orange whip, combine all ingredients in a food processor; blend until smooth. Serve chilled.
2. To make mango milkshake, place mango, ice and milk in blender or food processor, blend until smooth. Serve in tall glasses, decorate with a kiwi slice.

Serves 2 each drink

ingredients

orange honey whip

- **2 cups orange juice**
- **4 oranges, peeled and chopped**
- **2 tablespoons natural yogurt**
- **2 tablespoons honey**

mango milkshake

- **1 mango, peeled and stoned**
- **1 cup crushed ice**
- **1 cup milk**

tip from the chef

Excellent resources to add fresh fruit vitamins to children´s menu.

vanilla ice-cream

■□□ | Cooking time: 0 minute - Preparation time: 10 minutes

ingredients

- > 1/3 cup caster sugar
- > 1/3 cup water
- > 1 teaspoon gelatin
- > 2/3 cup milk powder
- > 2 cups milk
- > 1 teaspoon white vinegar
- > 2 teaspoons vanilla essence

method

1. Combine sugar and water in small saucepan, add gelatin, stir constantly over heat without boiling until sugar and gelatin are dissolved.
2. Transfer mixture to bowl, whisk in milk powder, then gradually beat in milk with electric mixer.
3. Pour into 2 lamington tins; cover with foil, freeze for about 1 hour or until almost set.
4. Transfer mixture to large bowl, add vinegar and essence, beat with electric mixer until thick and creamy. Return to lamington tins, cover, freeze for about 3 hours or overnight.

Makes about 1 1/2 liters/6 cups

tip from the chef

Great for ice-cream cones.

BETTA

frozen
banana nut iceblocks

a

■□□ | Cooking time: 5 minutes - Preparation time: 15 minutes

method

1. Peel bananas and cut in half (a). Insert wooden paddle pop sticks into each half (b).
2. Melt chocolate in a heatproof bowl over hot water. Remove from heat, add copha; mix well.
3. Brush each banana with chocolate mixture (c). Roll in chopped nuts (d), cover and freeze until serving.

Makes 10

ingredients

- **5 just-ripe bananas**
- **10 paddle pop sticks**
- **100 g/$3\frac{1}{2}$ oz dark chocolate**
- **15 g/$\frac{1}{2}$ oz copha, melted, or hydrogenated vegetable oil**
- **1 cup finely chopped peanuts**

tip from the chef

Paddle pop sticks will look very nice if dyed with edible food colorants of different tones. It is highly suggested to roast peanuts if you wish to make them more crunchy.

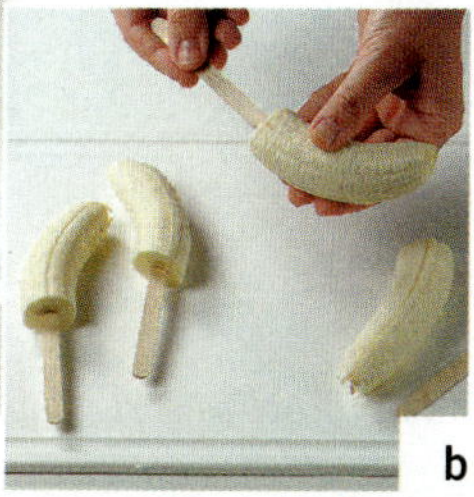

b

c

d

melon mousse

■□□ | Cooking time: 0 minute - Preparation time: 15 minutes

ingredients

- **5 cups chopped cantaloupe melon**
- **1/4 cup honey**
- **200 g/6 1/2 oz plain yogurt**
- **1 tablespoon gelatin**
- **2 tablespoons water**

method

1. Blend or process melon, honey and yogurt until smooth.
2. Sprinkle gelatin over water, dissolve over hot water (or microwave on High for about 20 seconds).
3. Stir gelatin mixture into melon mixture. Pour mixture into 4 serving dishes, refrigerate several hours or until set.

Serves 4

tip from the chef

Melon rind can be used as a bowl to serve the mousse.

frozen fruit balls

■□□ | Cooking time: 0 minute - Preparation time: 10 minutes

method

1. Using a melon baller, scoop out balls from watermelon, cantaloupe melon and honeydew melon.
2. Thread melon balls and grapes onto skewers and break off sharp ends.
3. Place on a foil covered tray, cover loosely with plastic food wrap and freeze for 3 hours or until frozen.

ingredients

- **1/4 watermelon**
- **1/2 cantaloupe melon**
- **1/2 honeydew melon**
- **250 g/8 oz seedless grapes**

Makes about 12

tip from the chef

Serve these fresh skewers with strawberry sauce; they are ideal for a Summer day.

sesame caramels

■■□ | Cooking time: 15 minutes - Preparation time: 15 minutes

ingredients

- > 3/4 cup sesame seeds
- > 1 cup brown sugar
- > 90 g/3 oz butter
- > 2 tablespoons honey
- > 1/3 cup liquid glucose
- > 1/2 cup sweetened condensed milk
- > 1/4 cup sunflower seeds, chopped

method

1. Place sesame seeds in frying pan and stir over a low heat until seeds are golden (a). Remove from pan to cool.
2. In a large saucepan, combine sugar, butter, honey, glucose and condensed milk (b), stir over low heat until sugar is dissolved, but not boiling. Slowly bring to the boil and cook uncovered for 7 minutes, stirring constantly.
3. Stir in 1/4 cup of toasted sesame seeds and sunflower seeds (c). Pour mixture into a foil-lined 29 x 19 cm/11 1/2 x 7 1/2 in lamington tin. Cool to room temperature.
4. Cut caramel into 4 strips lengthwise (d); fold each strip in half and roll into a log shape about 2 cm/3/4 in diameter (e). Roll each log in the remaining sesame seeds, refrigerate until ready to cut into slices.

Makes about 60

tip from the chef

It is important not to overcook the sesame, as it will get a bitter taste.

a

b

c

d

e

wheatmeal faces

■□□ | Cooking time: 0 minute - Preparation time: 10 minutes

method

1. Beat cream cheese in processor or electric mixer with lemon rind and sugar until smooth. Spread flat side of biscuits with cream cheese mixture.
2. Press 2 smarties and a jelly bean into cream cheese side to make a face. Allow to set for 30 minutes before serving.

Makes about 25

ingredients

- **1 packet wheatmeal biscuits**
- **250 g/$^{1}/_{2}$ lb packet cream cheese**
- **1 teaspoon grated lemon rind**
- **2 tablespoons icing sugar**
- **smarties**
- **jelly beans**

tip from the chef

Faces may be made up to 2 hours in advance.

index

Introduction 3

Early morning energy

Dried fruit salad with bananas 6
French toast 8
Fruity slice 12
Pikelet faces 10
Wholemeal shortbread 14

Nutritious lunches

Celery boats 24
Cheesy oat burgers 16
Fruity cheese log 22
Hi-fiber pasties 20
Pizza men 18

Family dinners

Chinese beef stir-fry 28
Mango chicken 30
Ocean perch in an oven bag 36
Pea and mushroom flan 44
Satay vegetables 46
Sesame coated chicken 34
Spicy apricot pork fillets 32
Tuna fish fingers 38
Veal with tomato and cheese 26
Vegeroni vegetable bake with cheese 40
Vegetable risotto 42

Nourishing and funny

Frozen banana nut iceblocks 54
Frozen fruit balls 58
Fruity drinks 50
Melon mousse 56
Sesame caramels 60
Vanilla ice-cream 52
Wheatmeal faces 62
Yogurt treats 48